POP HITS

FOR VIOLIN DUET

ALL OF ME

VIOLIN

Words and Music by JOHN STEPHENS
and TOBY GAD

Moderately fast

BRAVE

VIOLIN

Words and Music by SARA BAREILLES
and JACK ANTONOFF

D.C. al Coda

CODA

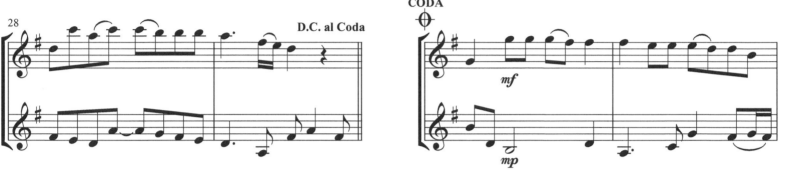

HEATHENS

VIOLIN

Words and Music by
TYLER JOSEPH

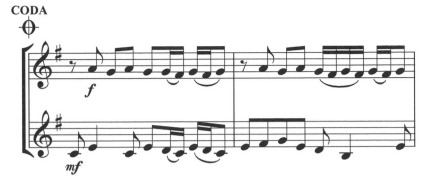

CODA

D.S. al Coda

HELLO

VIOLIN

Words and Music by ADELE ADKINS
and GREG KURSTIN

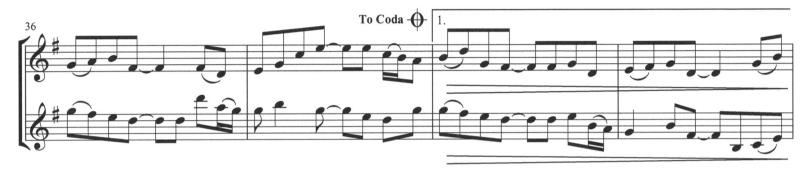

HOME

VIOLIN

Words and Music by GREG HOLDEN
and DREW PEARSON

I WILL WAIT

VIOLIN

Words and Music by
MUMFORD & SONS

D.S. al Coda
(take repeat)

CODA

Play 3 times

I'M NOT THE ONLY ONE

VIOLIN

Words and Music by SAM SMITH
and JAMES NAPIER

Slow jam

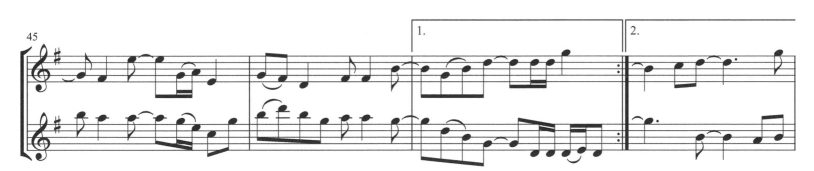

JUST THE WAY YOU ARE

VIOLIN

Words and Music by BRUNO MARS,
ARI LEVINE, PHILIP LAWRENCE,
KHARI CAIN and KHALIL WALTON

D.S. al Coda

CODA

LET IT GO
from FROZEN

VIOLIN

Music and Lyrics by KRISTEN ANDERSON-LOPEZ
and ROBERT LOPEZ

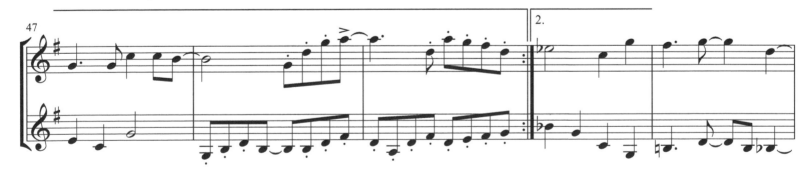

LET IT GO

VIOLIN

Words and Music by JAMES BAY
and PAUL BARRY

LITTLE TALKS

VIOLIN

Words and Music by
OF MONSTERS AND MEN

LOST BOY

VIOLIN

Words and Music by
RUTH BERHE

LOVE RUNS OUT

VIOLIN

Words and Music by RYAN TEDDER,
BRENT KUTZLE, ZACHARY FILKINS,
EDDIE FISHER and ANDREW BROWN

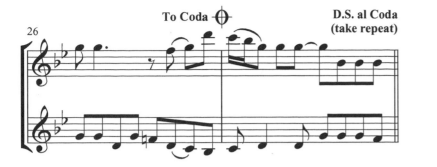

LOVE YOURSELF

VIOLIN

Words and Music by JUSTIN BIEBER,
BENJAMIN LEVIN and ED SHEERAN

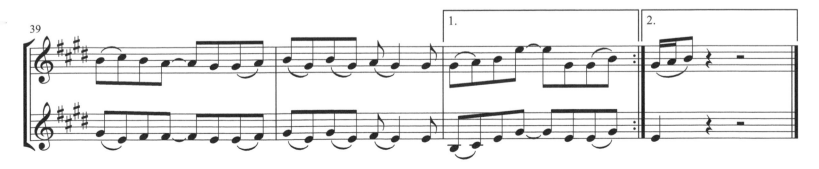

ONE CALL AWAY

VIOLIN

Words and Music by CHARLIE PUTH,
BREYAN ISAAC, MATT PRIME,
JUSTIN FRANKS, BLAKE ANTHONY CARTER
and MAUREEN McDONALD

D.S. al Coda

CODA

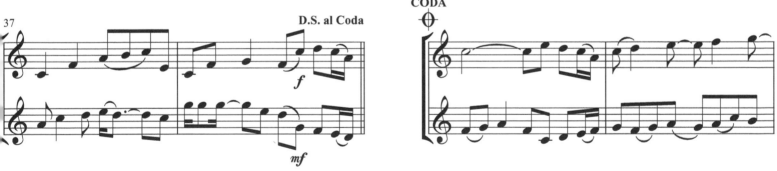

OPHELIA

VIOLIN

Words and Music by JEREMY FRAITES
and WESLEY SCHULTZ

Moderate half-time feel

PARADISE

VIOLIN

Words and Music by GUY BERRYMAN,
JON BUCKLAND, WILL CHAMPION,
CHRIS MARTIN and BRIAN ENO

Moderately fast, a feeling of 2

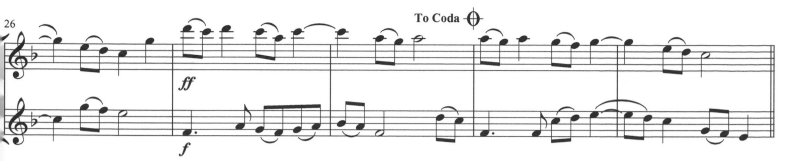

To Coda ⊕

1., 2. **3.**

D.S. al Coda **CODA** ⊕

RADIOACTIVE

VIOLIN

Words and Music by DANIEL REYNOLDS,
BENJAMIN McKEE, DANIEL SERMON,
ALEXANDER GRANT and JOSH MOSSER

To Coda ⊕

1.

2.

D.S. al Coda
(take repeat)

CODA
⊕

1.

2.

RIPTIDE

VIOLIN

Words and Music by
VANCE JOY

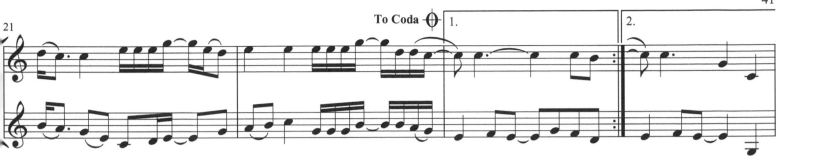

ROAR

VIOLIN

Words and Music by KATY PERRY,
MAX MARTIN, DR. LUKE,
BONNIE McKEE and HENRY WALTER

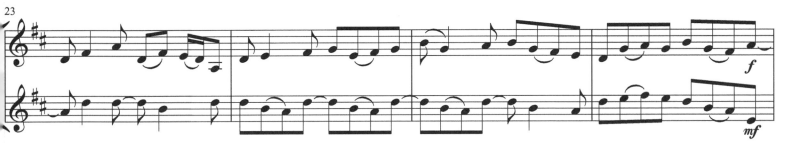

To Coda ⊕   D.S. al Coda   CODA ⊕

SAY SOMETHING

VIOLIN

Words and Music by IAN AXEL,
CHAD VACCARINO and MIKE CAMPBELL

7 YEARS

VIOLIN

Words and Music by LUKAS FORCHHAMMER,
MORTEN RISTORP, STEFAN FORREST,
DAVID LABREL, CHRISTOPHER BROWN
and MORTEN PILEGAARD

SHAKE IT OFF

VIOLIN

Words and Music by TAYLOR SWIFT,
MAX MARTIN and SHELLBACK

SKYFALL

from the Motion Picture SKYFALL

VIOLIN

Words and Music by ADELE ADKINS
and PAUL EPWORTH

Moderately slow

To Coda ⊕

D.S. al Coda

CODA
⊕

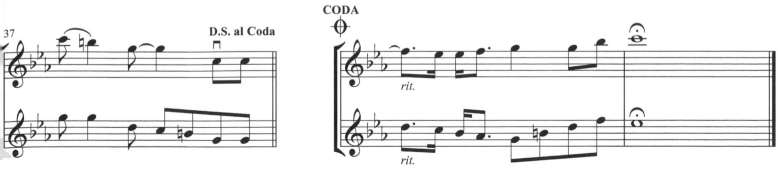

STORY OF MY LIFE

Violin

Words and Music by JAMIE SCOTT, JOHN HENRY RYAN,
JULIAN BUNETTA, HARRY STYLES, LIAM PAYNE,
LOUIS TOMLINSON, NIALL HORAN and ZAIN MALIK

Fast, in a driving 4

TAKE ME TO CHURCH

VIOLIN

Words and Music by
ANDREW HOZIER-BYRNE

Moderate Ballad

D.S. al Coda
(take repeat)

CODA

THINKING OUT LOUD

VIOLIN

Words and Music by ED SHEERAN
and AMY WADGE

WAKE ME UP!

VIOLIN

Words and Music by ALOE BLACC,
TIM BERGLING and MICHAEL EINZIGER

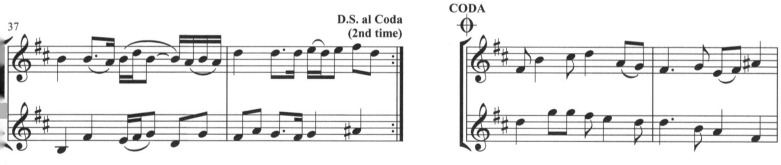

WE ARE YOUNG

VIOLIN

Words and Music by JEFF BHASKER,
ANDREW DOST, JACK ANTONOFF
and NATE RUESS

WE FOUND LOVE

VIOLIN

Words and Music by
CALVIN HARRIS

D.S. al Coda

CODA

VIOLIN DUET
COLLECTIONS

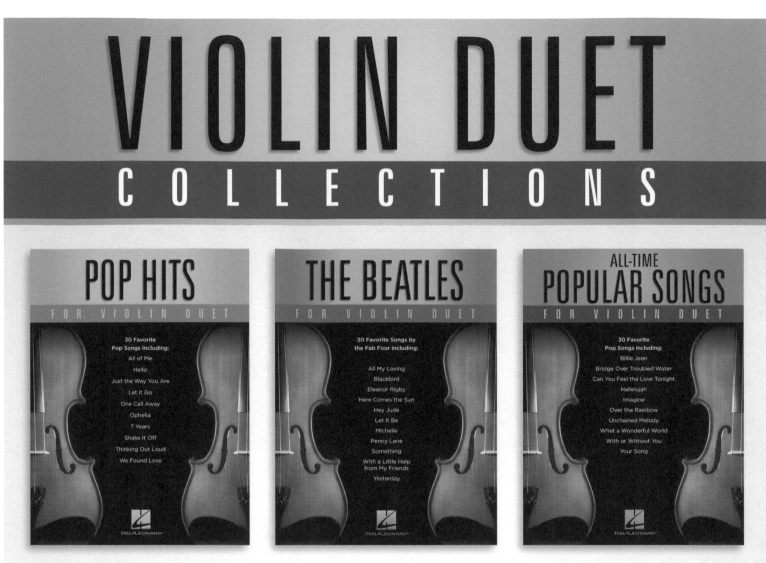

These collections are designed for violinists familiar with first position and comfortable reading basic rhythms. Each two-page arrangement includes a violin 1 and violin 2 part, with each taking a turn at playing the melody for a fun and challenging ensemble experience.

ALL-TIME POPULAR SONGS FOR VIOLIN DUET

Billie Jean • Bridge over Troubled Water • Can You Feel the Love Tonight • Hallelujah • Imagine • Over the Rainbow • Unchained Melody • What a Wonderful World • With or Without You • Your Song and more.

00222449 . . . . $14.99

THE BEATLES FOR VIOLIN DUET

All My Loving • Blackbird • Eleanor Rigby • A Hard Day's Night • Hey Jude • Let It Be • Michelle • Ob-La-Di, Ob-La-Da • Something • When I'm Sixty-Four • Yesterday and more.

00218245 . . . . $14.99

POP HITS FOR VIOLIN DUET

All of Me • Hello • Just the Way You Are • Let It Go • Love Yourself • Ophelia • Riptide • Say Something • Shake It Off • Story of My Life • Take Me to Church • Thinking Out Loud • Wake Me Up! and more.

00217577 . . . . $14.99

DISNEY SONGS FOR VIOLIN DUET

Beauty and the Beast • Can You Feel the Love Tonight • Colors of the Wind • Do You Want to Build a Snowman? • Hakuna Matata • How Far I'll Go • I'm Wishing • Let It Go • Some Day My Prince Will Come • A Spoonful of Sugar • Under the Sea • When She Loved Me • A Whole New World and more.

00217578 . . . . $14.99

www.halleonard.com

Prices, contents, and availability subject to change without notice.